WON
DER
LAND

WON DER LAND

ADVENTURES *in* DECORATING

SUMMER THORNTON

WITH ANTONIA VAN DER MEER

RIZZOLI
NEW YORK

New York · Paris · London · Milan

To Josh,
for always
dreaming
with me

contents

Introduction

One of my fondest memories from my childhood is when, every spring, the woods behind our house would erupt with millions of bluebells and become a sea of periwinkle blue. It was completely magical, and I'd skip through the bluebell-filled woods like they were my personal dream world. I have always been a dreamer. I'd put on plays; I'd dress up and pretend to be from another time; I'd practice foreign accents; I'd even decorate dollhouses with uncommon intensity. In my mind, I was always on some faraway journey. I was never really content with normalcy or everyday life, so instead I concocted ways to make it more fantastical.

"Let's embrace the magical moments, the fantasy, the fairy tale."

As an adult, I'm quite the same person. I don't take myself too seriously. I draw inspiration from an imaginary world. And now I get to help other people do the same with their homes. I want you to leave the mundane behind and follow me down the rabbit hole of your mind. Let's embrace the magical moments. Let's jump right in, headfirst, to live in a dream world of our own making.

If there's one thing I want you to take away from my book, it's to free yourself from decorating rules and the fear of what others will think. Be emboldened by what you see in these pages. Find your style and go for it with reckless abandon. Don't think about trends or this year's hottest colors. Never ask, "What am I *supposed* to like?" Just *do* what you like instead! Get off track, let your mind wander. The best ideas are sparked not out of necessity but by pure imagination. Allow yourself the freedom to express, to fail, and to experiment. It's your home, you make the rules.

I live to create. It's what gives me life and energy. Mixing color and pattern is my greatest talent, so I let it run wild. There are no limits when it comes to how many colors can be in one room or one scheme. Just keep going until it feels right. Add, layer, pile on the shades until you hit that sweet spot that makes your eye happy and your heart sing. Sometimes I audibly shriek when I nail a palette. I want to use the full crayon box of colors, and I don't believe in calling on neutrals to calm it down. I don't repeat colors or "pull" a color from the drapes to use on a pillow. Instead of falling in line, I'm going to show you how to design with unwavering confidence and color outside the lines to create a home that's refreshing and full of life. I hope my appetite for adventure is contagious and you catch it after reading this book.

My favorite part of any project is the very beginning, when anything is possible. I start with a story, typically some dream world I make up. The story unfolds into a palette and scheme. I am an instinctual designer. I do what feels right to me. It's messy at first, but soon I have a whole mood board of fabrics and images. I oftentimes can't sleep and will stay up all night thinking about it. I will lie in bed, staring at the ceiling, and imagine elevations of rooms and palettes coming together. It's the most intoxicating part of the job. I can see the final result down to the tiniest details. In the back of my mind, there's always a narrative when I am designing. It changes depending on who I'm writing the story for, but I continue to return to it throughout the project to keep it on track. There are a lot of distractions along the way, but my singular focus is always to tell the story in the most beautiful way possible.

In *Wonderland*, you'll see my own home in chapter 1 ("Fearless Romantic"), which reflects the sentimental side of my personality. This chapter is a love note to my family centered around the home we built together. Join me in chapter 3 ("Here Comes the Sun") on the sunny side of the street, where we peek into an over-the-top vacation home that's centered on citrus. You'll also see me misbehave a bit in chapter 5 ("It's Good to Be Bad"). This one is not for the faint of heart. If acting like a lady is more your cup of tea, I hope you see that we clean up quite nicely in chapter 2 ("The New Formal"), where you can tour some of our most polished pads to date. And finally, take a deep dive with me in chapter 4 ("Super-Saturated") through some of the most intensely colorful and joyful palettes we've ever explored. Put them all together and hopefully you get a little taste of the spectacular homes that we love to create.

With *Wonderland*, you can come with me through the looking glass into my Technicolor dream world. My houses are designed to transport you. So take that magic potion and let's go on an adventure together. Welcome to *Wonderland*.

11

1
fearless
romantic

"Why, sometimes I've believed as many as six impossible things before breakfast."

—LEWIS CARROLL, *THROUGH THE LOOKING-GLASS*

When it comes to interior design, reason, logic, and practicality are largely overrated. That's why I believe in decorating with the wildest abandon. Personal expression should be celebrated above all else. I am an escapist, and my home is where I retreat from reality—into a world of nickel tubs, marble fireplaces, whimsical textiles, surprising patterns, and secret gardens. Romanticism is sometimes pooh-poohed, but a little romance should be in everything one does. When you combine that soft, dreamy side of your personality with pure fearlessness, the result is untamed beauty. My mantra is simple. Do what you think is right, especially if it's something that has never been done before. Fortune favors the bold.

WELCOME TO MY HOME

The surest way to make a dream a reality is to identify it.

My husband, Josh, and I used to take long walks, fantasizing about living in one of Chicago's beautiful old Victorian homes. There was one house in particular that we had walked by for five years, and my love for it grew and grew. Finally, one day I had to say it out loud. "I want that white house!" I was six months pregnant at the time, so Josh did his best to indulge my insanity. It was an unlikely dream, to say the least, but two days later we saw a "for rent" sign in the window and immediately called to ask not if we could *rent* it but if we could *buy* it. It was wonderfully decrepit: paper peeling off the walls in huge swathes, pink '60s carpeting, orange Formica countertops. I'm pretty sure Josh saw nothing but a money pit. But as soon as the doors opened to the foyer, I saw only the dream.

Welcome to the world of my creation. My home perfectly encapsulates the two sides of my personality: the head and the heart. Though really, I tend to work with a double dose of heart. There is the inner world, where my heart is romantic, sensitive, and thoughtful, and the outer world, where I'm bold, confident, and unafraid. Let me throw open my doors and show you what I mean. I spent years dreaming and thinking, plotting and planning, buying and storing before we started renovating. The guiding principle was that everything we did – from removing and widening the back of the house to adding four fireplaces and French doors and replacing floors – had to look like it had always been there. It was a complete gut remodel, but we salvaged plaster ceiling medallions and painstakingly matched the profiles of moldings around doors and windows to the original ones. I worried that some things would look new, so much so that I took new marble floor tiles and had them hand-scooped to create long, arched divots – the exact effect that would have occurred if they had been walked on for hundreds of years.

ABOVE: If I had to leave my house forever and could only grab and save one thing, it just might be these beautifully bound marbleized-paper photo albums, filled with family pictures. I keep them within easy reach on my living room bookshelves, and they're my personal treasure. RIGHT: Textile choices mean everything to me. They are how most of my design work starts. Case in point: the silk brocade pillow on my mohair sofa.

"When you mix pop art with portraiture, it brings the dead back to life."

My favorite room is the living room. It took me forever to find the exact wall color I wanted. I had seen an ancient building on a Venice canal that haunted me (in a good way). It had a warm, perfect pink light reflecting off of it, and I decided *that* was the color I had to have. Being in the room always takes me back to that otherworldly city. We spend a lot of time here as a family, and the color warms everyone's skin tone and gives memories made there a rosy glow.

We added a wall of bookshelves because I am a hoarder and I wanted to display everything from classic old-world portraits to gorgeous coffee table books, bound marbleized-paper family photo albums, and childhood treasures. I love to surround myself with fresh flowers, shells, and coral fans. Living in awe of nature is part of what it means to be a romantic. But the incredible papaya-colored sofa with silk lilac fringe? That's just plain fearless.

PREVIOUS PAGES AND RIGHT: You want to know where we hang out? Here. Yes, the living room. Many people think a formal living room is a place where demure, proper, and polite people sit. Well, I'm not demure. And I don't let politeness get in my way. You won't find any precious, doll-size furniture in my house. Instead, I chose a big, deep down-filled sofa where I can sink in and relax with my family. The lady chairs from the '60s add a bit of levity—along with the '70s white molded plastic coffee table. I brightened and warmed this north-facing room with pinks, reds, oranges, and plums. The room is filled with things that are meaningful to me, like the squishy animal-print pillow that's on my sofa. It has followed me to many places and has sat on every sofa I've owned. It's like my pet.

ABOVE: I love my sofa with its intentionally mismatched lilac fringe. The walls are super soft, so I needed that hit of color. Where others might want to turn down the volume on color, I'm always busy turning it up. The mohair wool on my sofa is so luxurious, but also very forgiving and warm. If I had my way, I would put mohair on everything. RIGHT: On the weekends, you can find me sitting on this black floral chaise in my bay window. I try to sneak flowers in everywhere! I had planned to re-cover the chaise with another fabric because I wasn't sure about using black in the room, but when I saw how it looked there I changed my mind. If it works, it works. FOLLOWING PAGES: Part of being a romantic means being a collector—maybe even a bit of a hoarder! Josh and I collect old portraits and we use them everywhere. I love having a big place to display all my objects, including this fabulous shell box and some collected shells. You can't always have fresh flowers but you can always use shells for that much-desired nod to nature.

PREVIOUS PAGES: I needed my dining room to work with all kinds of colors, seasons, and party themes. I have tons of vibrant tablecloths and dinnerware that demand versatility. A neutral palette would be the standard solution, but of course that's not for me. Instead, I chose a wallpaper that has every color! It's much more flexible—and way more interesting. This scenic Gracie wallpaper emulates nature, with branches reaching up toward the sky. It's a chameleon. It looks light and verdant in the spring and summer. In the colder months, the silver leaf makes it look like a winter garden. ABOVE: When I thought about art, I knew I did not want to cover these glorious branches, so I opted for airy wall sconces (some plaster, some painted wood, and some porcelain). Now I can swap out flowers or objects at a moment's notice. The shelving creates a rotating accessory moment. RIGHT: The colorful high-back vintage chairs may not make much sense with the paper, but I fell in love with them anyway. The Tulu fabric is a dark blue–and–bright pink Japanese print, and even though it's not a high-performance fabric, it disguises all those "oops" moments—like when the kids get birthday cake on it.

"Practicality is the death of romance."

I don't ask for jewelry for Christmas. I ask for things like this French marble mantelpiece. Luckily for me, Josh is happy to oblige. The gift predates the architectural and design renovation of the house, and it waited a long time for a proper spot. Some of the best designs are created in reverse. Instead of looking at our kitchen and thinking what would work in the room, I look at a random piece like this seventeenth-century mantel and insist on making everything else in the room work around *it*. It's big—and takes up valuable real estate in a narrow townhouse—but I love the heft and the weight of it. There was no way I was going to be talked out of putting it there. It's a surprise to have a working fireplace in a kitchen, but it's great for added warmth on those cold Chicago nights. LEFT: The gigantic angel wings are carved from Mexican mesquite wood and covered in silver leaf. Josh and I found them on one of our trips to San Miguel de Allende. There's something wonderful about their presence in our house, and it feels like angels are watching over us as our family eats.

FAR LEFT, LEFT, AND ABOVE: You don't have to have white cabinets to have a bright kitchen. The mahogany-wood cabinetry adds a delicious dollop of French bistro polish. At first, I feared the antique marble fireplace made such a strong statement that I would have to settle for all-white countertops. But no! More marble—with plum veining—worked perfectly. The two mismatched marbles play off each other when used in the same room. The floral stripes on the kitchen chairs echo the Pierre Frey wallpaper used to back the living room bookshelves. The fabric is old and worn, and I may re-cover them someday, but for now, with two little kids, they're just right.

PREVIOUS PAGES, LEFT: This moody black vase with hand-painted flowers sits atop a messy stack of magazines. I always have about a two-foot pile of things I want to read next to my bed, almost all about interior design, but with a few parenting books thrown in. PREVIOUS PAGES, RIGHT: I feel pretty in this room. It's that simple. Poor Josh, he had no say here. It is an all-out feminine fantasy. Tucked away on the third floor, I think of it as my treetop escape. Honestly, I could live up here and do everything from my bed. ABOVE: A big mound of my daughter's stuffed animals temporarily migrated to my bed. My son saw them there and just had to dive into the pile. We love to snuggle up and read together. Homes are places where beautiful family memories can be captured forever in your mind. My design tries to foresee, and accommodate, those moments. RIGHT: This room is so layered with textiles. I used white picture molding around the tree of life Braquenié fabric wallcovering to give it a little breathing room and keep it from feeling heavy. I absolutely treasure the mash-up of cultures, from vintage Chiapas pillows to Russian floral-print fabrics and the suzani coverlet from central Asia at the end of the bed.

ABOVE AND RIGHT: My bathroom is (sort of) a family room. Many mornings, all four of us are happily in there together. So it makes sense that it would be big and welcoming. The gleaming nickel tub is the centerpiece and something I would not want to live without. The gas fireplace is modern—you can turn it on with the click of a button. I had this insane need to cover up that functionality (it ruins the dream) and eventually found a turn-of-the-century iron "summer cover." The fireplace looks like it belongs back in the 1870s—just like the large black, white, and plum marble tiles on the floor. Everything in the house has substance and weight and permanence. That's the way I like it. The plum veining in the cabochons lends extra romance. There's nothing bathroom-y about this bathroom.

ABOVE AND RIGHT: My little girl got the original main bedroom. Lucky her! It's an exaggerated, tall space, with soaring ceilings just high enough, I hope, to keep up with her dreams. When we first began the project, her favorite color was pink. Now it's blue, so I added this seventeenth-century wool needlepoint settee from the Paris flea in a bright cobalt. It's the perfect place for a cup of make-believe tea.

FAR LEFT AND ABOVE: A tiny bedroom for my little man. My son was named after the Sun King, and that was the inspiration for this bright golden-yellow room. Imagine a wood-paneled gentleman's den, but in the brightest of colors—with a Russian red carpet on the floor, bright yellow glossy bookcases, and hidden closets. LEFT: The playroom's walls are wrapped in a cheery William Morris floral print. Much to his delight, my son only recently noticed the Fornasetti clouds on the ceiling. Even after living here for two years, he's still finding surprises and new things that catch his eye. That's the joy of layers. Whimsy is the lifeblood of my design. It keeps things fresh, modern, and real. There's so much to see around you—and above you. Let the fun begin!

"Every day can be a fantasy when you create a dream world."

RIGHT: No garden room is complete without plenty of wicker, big, blousy floral fabrics, and a classic pedestal for displaying something powerful, like this oversize Chinese vase of branches.

FOLLOWING PAGES: The renovations to our home were so extensive that we were able to create spaces like this garden room that didn't even exist before. We tore off the back of the house entirely! That's what allowed us to expand this room and have these marvelous French doors to the garden and dramatic fireplaces throughout. Of course, I went to painstaking efforts to ensure that it all felt original. We had to plan for it carefully before the demolition and renovation even began! I spent lots of time calculating the size of the French doors, the depth needed for the pocket shutters, the dimensions for casements that would match those original to the house, and the width of the chimney. It was like a Rubik's Cube of planning to ensure perfect spacing. I know that sounds nerdy, but it's necessary for getting everything right. Now when you look at this garden room, all you see is the dream.

ABOVE: These pillows are a fun collection, including a classic old world chintz, a traditional Scalamandré tiger print, and then a Thai batik fabric thrown into the mix to loosen things up a bit. RIGHT: The trellis, placed over boxwood-green walls, makes you wonder whether you are really inside after all. It's a total Victorian fantasy full of ferns, flowers, and latticework. FOLLOWING PAGES, LEFT: Josh and I are so happy to have outdoor space in the city. It's a place to breathe, to play, and to party. A garage with an in-law apartment encloses the space and offers almost complete privacy. FOLLOWING PAGES, RIGHT: A Grecian face makes the perfect planter. PAGES 60-61: I dreamed of having a New Orleans–inspired garden with marble flagstones. But marble couldn't withstand Chicago winters, so we sourced limestone and granite from northern Europe and Asia and had it cut extra thick to withstand freezing temperatures without cracking. Practicality does have its place, but I never start with it!

Life of the Party

I live to throw a party. And this house is perfect for it, thanks to my secret garden just downstairs from the kitchen and off the garden room. When I host, I think about it like I am telling a story or setting a scene for a movie. I love a theme, and I often ask guests to come in costume. I can be a bit extra – I've accepted that. But I do it so that my guests can enter another world. Of course, even though I am taking them on a trip down the rabbit hole, I still want them to feel comfortable. I want them to stay and stay. It's not a good party if people go home before 2:00 a.m.! Once I threw a *Midsummer Night's Dream* party. I covered the tables with moss, we all wore floral headpieces, I placed candles everywhere, I put out giant boards laden with cheeses and fruits. A tattooed harpist with blue hair played ethereal music from the balcony above the garden.

PREVIOUS PAGES: White brick walls topped with antique terra-cotta, black iron chairs, and custom-made cast iron railings from New Orleans all help carry me off to another time and place. ABOVE LEFT: Rich green cabbage plates, amber dotted glass, and a parrot figurine make for a lively table. ABOVE RIGHT: Things are really looking up when you have a ceiling full of shiny helium balloons. RIGHT: There's a tablecloth out there for every occasion, like this one, which I had made from an Indian block print. I hoard them, knowing that each one will eventually find its moment center stage. String lights always up the romance in the evening.

2
the new formal

"'Yes, that's it,' said the Hatter with a sigh: 'it's always tea-time.'"

—LEWIS CARROLL, *ALICE'S ADVENTURES IN WONDERLAND*

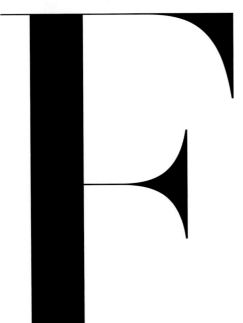

For some of my clients, only the utmost in formality will do, and I'm all for it. Formal may seem like a safe choice, but it's actually its own form of rebellion—rebellion against today's casualness and I-can't-be-bothered attitude. These clients eschew false humility and embrace the unapologetic fantasy of living like royalty. Don't be fooled by their Chanel suits. A wild heart beats underneath. It's not about what everyone else is doing. It's about what they want: silver-leaf ceilings, gilded mirrors, silk velvet where one should never put silk velvet, and china on the table every day. I'm proud to help bring artisanship back, filling these storied homes with hand-cast metals, and mouth-blown glass. I happily go against the grain to embrace the fabulous freedom of utter lavishness.

Right off the kitchen, with a lovely view of the grounds and pool, the garden room awaits. This is where the couple eats most nights, with gorgeous light and fresh air thanks to huge windows and French doors. This is not your typical garden room. There are no rattan chaises or wicker chairs, and no chintz in sight. Although the room is light and breezy and full of ferns, the furniture we used is strong and weighty. A brass-trimmed yacht table with massive pedestals serves as the dining table and is surrounded by leather chairs. It's a solid anchor for such an airy space.

BLACK TIE OPTIONAL

Formality doesn't have to be restrictive. It can be fun. That's why we pushed it to extremes in every direction in this magnificent home – from heavenly sunlit rooms to sultry, moody, inky rooms on the other end of the spectrum. There is no middle ground for me.

With big houses come big dreams. We let our imaginations run wild in this manse. We had so many rooms in which to indulge our design fantasies! We dove right in, creating one exquisite movie-worthy set after another. We studied old films, vintage train cars, and five-star European hotels. Every room was given a strong personality of its own. But there is one room in particular – the office for the woman of the house – that is a particular favorite of mine. It has a deeply moody, wintry palette of Prussian blues, sapphires, and silvers. I think Russian royalty would feel right at home here. I was inspired by the beauty of the Venice Simplon-Orient-Express and channeled that vibe with rich materials and plush textiles that bring you to an elevated place in your mind, allowing for an escape from the ordinary. Who knows where this room will take you or how long you will be gone? Even the rugs underfoot are luxurious, spun in pale silver silk. A frosted blue Murano glass lamp encapsulates everything I was thinking of during the design – otherworldly elegance, an icy light, a sexy color. This office is far from ordinary and was designed to offer a much-deserved escape from the real world.

Traditional homes typically have a reserved palette, but that doesn't mean we were going to choose timid colors. I prefer shades that are intense and stirring. Where a gray sofa might have been expected, I chose a lapis blue sofa instead. Rich details like horsehair upholstery, hand embroidery, hanging tassels, and silver

ABOVE: The posh pedestals for the ferns were originally designed to be uplights, but we turned them into planters. They fit nicely inside the windows and are the one sure sign that you are in a garden room. RIGHT: I love the architectural elements present throughout. The pillars and the arches seem to stand guard over the whole room. A giant globe-shaped lantern hangs from the ceiling, grabbing your attention and demanding respect. It looks like something that should be in the lobby of an old Wall Street bank. But we used it here in the most casual room of the house to add drama and a little tension. The terra cotta–tile floor is almost completely covered. We topped it with a flat-woven wool rug and then added a knotted plush rug on top with a modern, abstract pattern. The layered look helps separate the dining area from the sitting area. A white chair with exposed wood-frame arms and an Art Deco–inspired camel leather ottoman are inviting places to sit and relax before or after dinner. The leather helps add a sense of casualness to this family space. The walls are grass cloth, giving texture and warmth to a room that, because of its size and tile floor, might otherwise feel cold.

"Whimsy should be allowed to wander in through an open door."

leaf all transport you back in time. Baccarat chandeliers, printed velvets, a leather-wrapped desk, and bronze-capped chairs are just some of the ways we tell the story of opulence and refinement in this house. But I couldn't just leave it at that. I created some tension between refinement and drama by taking the tasteful and the traditional and juxtaposing it against something that shakes things up a bit, like an animal print or an unexpected color. That's what gives this grand residence the modernity it craves. It helps the design feel fresh among all the traditional notes.

From the moment you enter this house, the experience is immersive, with monochromatic tonal shades working together in every room to create an elevated, dramatic, European feel. My client asked me to err on the side of formality, and I embraced that desire wholeheartedly. I think if you're going to do something, you should lean all the way in. Yet for all its formality, there's nothing stiff or untouchable here. The sofas are deep and the fabrics feel good on the skin. It's a pampered, pretty way to live. A world you can feel very good waking up in – as long as you are wearing the right pajamas. Silk ones, of course.

All the furniture is structural and masculine—from the navy leather–and-brass dining chairs to the sleek, sophisticated sofa—but because it's a garden room at heart, I wanted to add a moment of levity. A bronze sculpture with a sheepskin body is the perfect touch and makes everyone smile. The floral pillow on the sofa and a chartreuse throw are clear nods to the garden. The sofa is a modern interpretation of an Art Deco–era tuxedo sofa, with arms the same height as the back. It's covered in a blue-gray mohair and piped in navy leather. This is one sophisticated garden room!

ABOVE: What could be more opulent than velvet-covered walls? And why not keep the unbridled decadence going with luminous silver and gold–brocade drapes? They look like fabulous ball gowns waiting to be worn to a party. The sconces are incredibly elegant and perfectly in proportion to the tall, narrow room. Tiny caged silk shades sit atop, lending a finishing touch as perfect as a poem. RIGHT: A blue-gray leather-wrapped desk is the ideal place for writing an elegantly penned thank-you note. Notably missing: all the usual detritus of daily living. (Messy files, unused envelopes, and black staplers? All neatly tucked away in drawers and a workhorse closet.)

ABOVE AND RIGHT: This garden-inspired bathroom, off the blue-velvet office, was led by a glorious hand-painted Gracie wallpaper. Silver clamshell sconces are a favorite of mine, so naturally I found a place for them here. I left instructions that they should be allowed to tarnish because I think things that are slightly less than perfect feel more alive. Blue Calacatta marble on the floor and the vanity looks cool, calm, and collected. Light pours in through floor-to-ceiling windows. The framed Damien Hirst butterfly art on the wall is iridescent and delightfully changes color with the changing light.

LEFT: Waking up in this bedroom is like waking up in a suite at the Ritz in Paris. It is so buttoned up and decadent at the same time. The silver-leaf beds have green silk velvet headboards and footboards. They look antique. The Pierre Frey shades have an embroidered velvet trim. Every wall is covered in silk, a distinctly elegant look that easily elevates any room. The Empire-style dressers are exquisite, with gold fluting and a step detail, while the gilded wavy mirror takes the dressers down a notch. Like Noah's ark, everything in this room goes marching two by two with its mate; we made sure that everything is perfectly paired. There are two beds, two dressers, two mirrors, two benches. ABOVE: The adjoining bathroom has an old European look. The deep soaking tub and the printed damask on cotton drapes are so romantic! I love the shape of the sconce. Its projection is so deep, it creates a very lovely profile. Having tiny shades that match the drapes is a cheeky finish.

"If you've got it, flaunt it. Better yet— gild it."

RIGHT AND FOLLOWING PAGES: This bedroom is like a decadent piece of pecan pie: indulgent and rich! The success of a copper-colored bedroom was the biggest surprise to me. I've always said that I love all colors, but brown isn't my most frequent companion. This was the first time I decorated a room with it as the dominant shade. And do you know what? It's glorious! One of the reasons a dark hue works is because the room itself is so full of light. Add to that pale silver silk carpeting and shiny metallics, and you create a crisp contrast to the cinnamon tones. Everything in this bedroom has weight and substance: the drapes are a soft, peachy cut velvet; the armoire is made of saddle leather and solid brass; the chairs are silk velvet; and other furniture is a rich mahogany. The large-scale Murano sunburst light fixture is incredibly striking. It looks like spears of ice.

ABOVE: The silk velvet headboard is a rich amber. An antique marble-topped chest makes an impressive bedfellow. RIGHT: Deep, rich-colored sofas and club chairs create a kind of hush that invites you to retreat into a quieter world. You feel like the most elegant version of yourself in this room. Gold touches are right at home amid the silks and the velvets. Horsehair on an oval ottoman cues the owners' love of all things equestrian.

"A purple sofa is a real power move."

RIGHT: Looking into the gentleman's office from the outside is like peeking into the pages of an eighteenth-century novel. It feels very British, traditional, and posh with its giant limestone fireplace and knotty pine paneling. Naturally, we played against type by choosing a magnificent intense violet Loro Piana cashmere sofa backed by a bronze-and-glass console table for books (yes, more books!). FOLLOWING PAGES: The modernist Murano glass fixture is enormous, stunning, and slightly inappropriate. It provides the perfect contrast to the classic pine walls, while simultaneously mimicking the shape of the turret that houses the built-in desk. The frieze above the bookshelves is a Fornasetti cloud print, creating an imaginative topper. The sofa is curved to follow the shape of the nine-foot-long marble coffee table that sits in front of it. It took nine men to get this outrageously heavy table in place, but it was worth the effort. The scale of the room demands a modern piece this size. This room is striking and powerful!

LEFT: The owners of this home are big book lovers. They each have thirty-five books on their bedside tables alone! Leather-bound antique books spill out from every shelf in his office. The interest in this room comes from the contrast between the formal and traditional vibes versus the more modern ones. We added some quirky colors—reds and plums and purples—to the fabric on the club chairs. ABOVE: This bar is well suited to the man of the house. It's timeless for sure, but with a lot of edge. There is a background of perfect pine joinery and well-bound leather books, but it's layered with a stepped-brass '70s Italian lamp and an in-your-face sculpture made of powder-coated nails that's almost three feet tall. It sucks any stuffy air right out of the room. Perfect for a man who steps to his own irreverent beat and doesn't know the meaning of the word can't.

95

Past Perfect

I use vintage pieces as liberally as possible because they really grab you. They take you out of the ordinary and out of your comfort zone to a place in time where people thought differently. Sourcing vintage is exhilarating to me. I find inspiration in the history and the stories. A piece like this modernist Murano glass fixture can spark an idea for an entire room. Vintage lighting is always a must for me, but I don't stop there. I'll go as far as I'm allowed. From Chinese Art Deco rugs to vintage Venetian mirrors, the more vintage used, the merrier the tone. Sometimes when vintage just isn't practical due to scale or function, we use it as a jumping-off point for custom pieces. The bottom line: if it's old, I fall hard. I hope you can see the beauty in these rare lighting finds, even if my electrician cannot!

LEFT: Two incredible vintage lamps stand tall on the console table. I love the combination of the yellow sphere and the amethyst Murano glass in the base. We updated the look with a simple black paper shade. ABOVE LEFT: This early nineteenth-century Chinese Art Deco rug is an amazing vintage piece. Known as a zodiac rug, it features all twelve animals—from dragons and pigs to monkeys. Because of its age and use, the rug looks distressed, and that's what I love about it. Vintage rugs often feature deep colors and intricate designs. ABOVE RIGHT: The gentleman who uses the study is a tinkerer with a scientist's curiosity. The fixture reminds me of the intricate inner workings of an old clock, and so it seemed to match his personality.

HEAD IN THE CLOUDS

This amazing apartment was a love gift for a wife whose dream is to live in the greatest refinement and sophistication. We indulged her desire for all things formal and pushed that idea right to the brink. The result: palace perfection with a modern twist. This place is proper with a capital *P*, just the way she likes it.

Most of the apartments in this landmarked Art Deco building were remodeled to be contemporary, but we took things in a different direction. We started by adding architectural touches like crown moldings and wall moldings, cornice details, and built-in cabinetry. Everything had to be impeccable. If we're going to go formal, let's be excessively formal. Start by silver-leafing everything. Roll out the silk carpets and panel every wall imaginable. Polish the dark brown floors in the living room to a high sheen. You will know right away that you are somewhere dressy – a place where delicate, light-reflecting silk velvet fabrics don't seem impractical at all! A place where you can head to bed in silk pajamas and wake up to breakfast served on fine china in an exquisite kitchen.

I like clients who are brave enough to fully own who they are and go for it. I like to pull out all the stops and let them live like royalty. But I am always going to be fearless in my approach and my use of color. For this apartment, we chose a watery palette with shades of periwinkle and aqua that blend into one another rather than pop. It sparks newness because it's a pale wash of hues. This home is all about light and reflection. The living room is an airy, cloudlike fantasy...if clouds were made of silver leaf, that is!

"Live like Marie Antoinette is coming to breakfast."

The overall style is precise and tailored, but always with a wink to whimsy. I never lose sight of that, even in the most buttoned-up rooms. The exotic dragons, Staffordshire dog figurines seated on wall pedestals, and a chartreuse chandelier keep things lighthearted. An alabaster globe hanging from the ceiling is a quiet touch that doesn't boast its own beauty too loudly. Even the grand floor in the entry is formal and playful at the same time. Nero Marquina and Carrara marbles are the most classic of choices, but the playful circles and exaggerated scale in proportion to the small space put a whole new spin on things. It reminds me of a giant tic-tac-toe board. Exaggeration of scale is a key element that recurs in most of my designs. Many of the furnishings we chose neatly echo the era of the building – like a stunning 1940s vintage mirror that steps in, referencing the Art Deco stairs of the building, or a silk brocade chair with fluted arm details.

Living here, it's easy to get carried away.

PREVIOUS PAGES: The dark blue (almost black) color on the walls helps to turn this pass-through into an actual room. With so many openings, it needed a strong, dark color to make you feel enveloped in the space. We added built-in shelves for the owner's collection of antique books. A chair with caning details and a worn caramel-colored leather seat mimics the look of the book bindings. And a surprising chartreuse chandelier is there as a wake-up call—proper manners are important, but nobody should have to be on good behavior all the time. RIGHT: A classic Pierre Frey wallpaper looks insanely cozy in this kitchen. Pattern always makes me feel at ease, and if that's not enough, the fireplace flanked by bookshelves would make anyone feel right at home. FOLLOWING PAGES: The window seat is so comfortable, you could work here, eat here, stay here all day drinking tea. The hanging brass-and-glass shelving allows the owner to display a collection of antique glassware, porcelains, and silver services—a mix of inherited and collected pieces. There's an airiness to an island when it is not solid. This one is a reproduction of an antique farm table. Big baskets underneath serve as drawers. We liked what we saw in a Parisian bar and kept that look in mind by using floating shelves. A classic black hood with strapping is a natural contrast to the white subway tiles.

Hall Monitor

Can we all come together to banish long, dark hallways, please? Let's replace them with hallways that add life and joy to our homes. Keep in mind that hallways can be major arteries to your world, so don't lose the mood here. Lackluster hallways rudely wake you from the dream that has been so carefully created in the rest of the house. Well-designed hallways keep you entranced. They romance you. They lead you toward the light. One of my favorite tricks is to brighten hallways by using a high-gloss lacquer treatment on the walls because it bounces light around. Don't be shy. Make a statement. Cover the walls from floor to ceiling with artwork or family photos. Don't stop there. Pay attention to the hallway floor. It's a great excuse for drama. A patterned floor can really pick up the pace and delight your eye from one end to the other. Likewise, barrel-vault ceilings and other architectural details can elevate a run-of-the-mill hallway from drab to delightful. Demand a hallway that doesn't just *get* you there, it *takes* you there.

LEFT: An unusually long hallway demands a bold graphic floor. A pair of antique mahogany tables with bronze inlays and marble tops are certainly living room–worthy, but they're not even a little bit wasted in a hallway. The lavish furnishings make it more than just a path to something else. This hallway is an adventure all its own. ABOVE LEFT: Arches and exaggerated paneling lead you on a magical mystery tour ABOVE RIGHT: This hallway, with its shiny lacquered walls, doubles as an art gallery. The client owned lots of art and had a keen interest in displaying it, so we created a floating shelf system to allow for a rotating gallery. Now she is never bored and can move pieces around to wondrous effect. There's nothing better than a dramatic hallway to take you from one dream space to another!

3

here comes the sun

"'But what am I to do?'
said Alice. 'Anything you like,'
said the Footman..."
—LEWIS CARROLL, *ALICE'S ADVENTURES IN WONDERLAND*

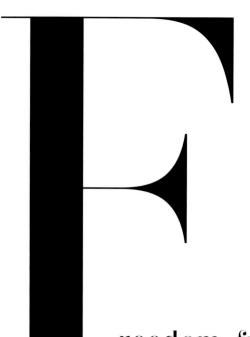

An island vibe is amplified by an antique mahogany bench with a beautiful rush seat. The giant tin mirror behind it was custom made in Mexico for this space. The silver color blends in nicely with the silver leaf wallpaper. What's really cool is the mix of the formal, baroque shape of the mirror with the informal tin material—and the contrast of the wood and the rush against the silver leaf. It all adds up to one of my favorite little moments. The sconces on either side of the mirror are fantastic. It's hard to beat a wooden-shell backplate with green hurricane glass.

Freedom, frivolity, joy, light, abandon— these are the things that influence my design of vacation homes. Such places are necessary escapes where dreams can run wild and free. My clients are perhaps more open to *possibility* here than anywhere else. In their second homes, they have license to embrace a different side of their personalities. Sun and the sea make everyone feel happier, sexier, freer. My interpretation of their fantasies includes warm rattans, cool silver leaf, playfully outrageous hand-painted wall-paper, delicious citrus colors—and even cashmere and leather where you'd least expect it. The goal is to tell a story, play make-believe, and set a scene previously unseen. Does that sound a little absurd? Then we're on the right track.

PREVIOUS PAGES AND RIGHT: The lounge chairs are neatly lined up with matching lemon-drop pillows against a backdrop of dark green hedges, giving the pool area an exclusive, resort-like feel. The symmetry and restraint belie a wilder, more energetic élan inside the main house. FOLLOWING PAGES: Sometimes it can take a while to move from the real world to a vacation mindset. Not here. The minute you enter, you are thrown into the deep end of your imagination—surrounded by four walls of metallic de Gournay wallpaper with giant Japanese koi fish and an intricately carved center table. There is an immediate wow factor that flies you a million miles away from wherever you were before. A foyer should be the opening scene of your dream.

HELLO, YELLOW

Whimsical umbrellas were the jumping-off point for this story. Made from vintage fabrics and pieced together to form a patchwork, they reference a simpler time. The pool takes on an intentionally nostalgic vibe. I live in the past in my mind and wanted this property to celebrate a golden age of beauty and leisure. My clients bought this Florida getaway on a whim, and they approached the decorating of it with great joy. They feel so happy and fortunate to own it.

Best of all, *no* was not in their vocabulary. Giant Japanese koi fish on a hand-painted de Gournay wallpaper in the entry? Oh, yes! Metallic surfaces? Goatskin ashtrays? Yes and yes. Rococo-shape tin mirrors? Why not? Lemon, lime, and tangerine? Definitely! There was no stopping our bright, airy, fanciful march through this house. The ceilings are high, and the house is drenched in sunlight. Open-concept spaces can be challenging (and truthfully, they are not my favorite). It's important to rein in the space, create tonal moments, and set intimate scenes to add interest.

As soon as you open the doors, you're transported. The house completely wraps you in a vacation fantasy. Actually, *two* fantasies – his and hers. *He* longed for formality and elegance. *She* gravitated toward the light, whimsical, and informal. Of course, they both got their dream in the end (I wouldn't allow for anything less), and that's what makes their home truly magical. I paired an intricately carved 1700s table from the Philippines with

ABOVE: The Picasso-esque vase embodies the whole aesthetic of this house. It is a great piece of art, but it doesn't take itself too seriously. We gave it to the family as a gift when the house was finished. My method (or is it madness?) makes sure nothing feels too heavy. RIGHT: The dining room is open to the living room and therefore needed its own voice. Luckily, the shell-shaped plaster chandelier truly sings. And the Hunt Slonem painting of tropical parrots (a gift from the client's brother) helps to define and separate this space from the rest of the house.

"When life gives you lemons, decorate with fruit."

handwoven abaca rugs. I updated antique hurricanes with backplates that look like seashells. A little formal, a little fun. I covered wood and cane chairs with palm-print fabrics. The mistake in a beach house is to go too light and bright on everything. You need some grounding pieces of furniture to add substance and permanence. I always want the pieces in a home to look acquired over time – not assembled all at once from one source.

Happily, my clients' seemingly opposite dreams turned out to be the perfect pairing. Like the umbrellas by the pool, the patchwork created by their multiple parts achieves a more satisfying whole. The house is a shiny reflection of their love and good humor toward each other and their guests – of which there is an endless stream. The house became so completely irresistible that it rose to be more than a vacation place, and the couple decided to move in permanently. A fairy-tale ending. In paradise, no less.

RIGHT: The whole palette for the house is based on citrus. This is Florida, after all. And yellow is my clients' favorite color. Savor the lemon yellows, intense oranges, and vivacious limes throughout. The trick to making sure the fruit theme doesn't get kitschy is the juxtaposition of high and low. Yes, it's fruit. But it's also Dalí. Have no fear of the ordinary—as long as you make it extraordinary. FOLLOWING PAGES: We all fell in love with this fanciful hand-painted tropical-patterned wallpaper and knew it had to go somewhere. But where? The kitchen was not the obvious choice. So of course that's the room we chose! In a fit of fancy, we decided to use it as the backsplash, which meant it had to be covered in glass. This was no easy feat, but it was worth it. The masculine caramel-colored leather barstools are a nice counterpoint. They allow a little cigar-smoking, men's-club atmosphere to brush up against an otherwise airy, resort-style backdrop.

ABOVE: Make no mistake, this is a real working kitchen and not some precious showpiece for voyeurs. The lady of the house's brother is a chef. The couple owns restaurants, and everyone loves to cook. Thus, the giant 56-inch Lacanche range, handcrafted in France, was a must-have. RIGHT: I prefer the aura of impracticality, even though I also secretly like things to be practical. So I kept the hardworking parts of the kitchen largely hidden from view. The latticework cabinetry neatly camouflages the refrigerator, freezer, and a floor-to-ceiling cabinet, chock-full of dishware and entertaining essentials. FOLLOWING PAGES, LEFT: Fish and coral themes add to the fun. FOLLOWING PAGES, RIGHT: You need brown wood to give a light, bright beach house permanence. The oak paneling looks rich and adds a sense of refinement.

PREVIOUS PAGES: The bedroom is an all-out fantasy. I pushed the limit with yellow wool cashmere drapes and a scenic lemon-grove panorama from Gracie covering the walls. ABOVE AND RIGHT: The four-poster bed and the nude leather sofa are delicate touches that bring romance to the room. The scalloped detail on the bed linens is both beachy and formal. FOLLOWING PAGES: The armoire with inlaid mother-of-pearl is a stunner. I love this room. I can't think of a better place for rest and relaxation, not to mention the fact that you get to wake up every morning in your own private tropical paradise.

"Natural wood + citrus colors = tropical happiness."

I never design bathrooms like they are bathrooms. To me, they can be so much more. His-and-hers sinks are tucked into individual niches with oak-wood vanities, wearing blue Calacatta marble tops, composed of fluted details and gold shell knobs. Creamy limestone floor tiles mixed with gray-blue marble and dark brown cabochons create a satisfying pattern that grounds everything. The mirrors double as hidden TVs for a needed news fix first thing in the morning. You can't see them, but they're there. There are no secrets between a designer and her clients—especially in the bathroom.

LEFT: You almost never see drapes in a bathroom, but I love them because they bring you back into a dream world. And that's where I think one should live. Practicality bores me. Wherever there is straight-up utility, I push back with something beautiful and surprising. Never settle for less. Good design can do both. ABOVE: A small round brass table adds a surprisingly gracious touch usually reserved for a living room.

ABOVE AND RIGHT: We certainly did not hold ourselves back in the main bedroom, but if it's possible, we felt even freer to let ourselves go in the guest bedrooms. Hand-blocked batik fabrics line the walls and repeat and echo throughout the room, landing on the lampshades and the canopy bed and bouncing over to the window treatments. I love the way they highlight the soaring height of the ceilings, while at the same time enveloping you in a womb-like feeling of comfort and warmth.

"Why try to pretend that decorating is *effortless*? Drop the façade. Go all out!"

Being on vacation means leaving your usual world behind and entering a whole different headspace. I wanted the tabletop to take you away to an exquisite old-world island era. The Indian block-print fabric was an inexpensive find that we used as a tablecloth. Its cheerfulness is contagious. The rattan sleeves for the glasses, the woven place mats, and the bamboo flatware are nostalgic and whimsical. The plate is in a chinoiserie pattern that is echoed throughout the house.

ABOVE: A bowl full of bright, round limes doubles as a colorful centerpiece at a party. But you can still grab one for your drink. RIGHT: There's no need to draw a line between indoor and outdoor living spaces when you entertain in a warm-weather locale. We kept the lemon yellows going strong from the pillows on the pool chaises and sofas to the seat cushions on the cane dining room chairs.

Looking Up

If I see a surface, I have to cover it – and that includes ceilings. I always need more color and more pattern. I'm a maximalist. And I like surprises. The ceiling is there for the taking. It completes the picture, adds another layer, and is one more way to catch the eye. Why pass up a chance to add more beauty and interest to a room's design? I don't think people realize how much they tend to look up when they come into a space. Having a finished ceiling expands your horizons. Putting pattern on a ceiling is especially important when the ceiling is low. It may seem counter-intuitive: although you might think it would be oppressive, it has the opposite effect, as the ceiling becomes more experiential. You're going to feel how low it is anyway, so you might as well go for it and amplify the experience. The other thing I love to do is to use lacquered paint on ceilings. White lacquer reflects the light and gives you that light-as-air feeling, particularly when the room's windows face water.

PREVIOUS PAGES AND LEFT: This is the tale of a sad little room above the garage with lots of tiny windows and no personality. Challenge accepted. Look at it now! It is a chic tentlike space with three individual niches for beds and an additional trundle bed below each. Now guests fight to stay in this room. ABOVE LEFT: Striped paper on the walls leads the eye up to floral paper on the ceiling in this old-school foyer. The table is large enough to host overflow guests at a dinner party, without the slightest worry of complaints that they were relegated to the kids' table. ABOVE RIGHT: Vintage Brunschwig & Fils geometric paper with a Mondrian vibe gives this living room some serious creative cred.

4
super saturated

"'How do you know I'm mad?' said Alice. 'You must be,' said the Cat, 'or you wouldn't have come here.'"

—LEWIS CARROLL, *ALICE'S ADVENTURES IN WONDERLAND*

W

I find things I love, such as this mirror of recycled industrial parts, and I see how they can work together with other pieces I curate for a project. It's a puzzle. I appreciate the way something as formal as nineteenth-century wood paneling can be reimagined, simply by forgoing a more traditional gilded mirror in favor of a younger, edgier piece. Meanwhile, a wooden Regency desk introduces natural wood, an important counterpoint in a space that is so fiercely saturated.

hen it comes to color, I am full steam ahead. Full throttle. No stops. The more extreme, the more experimental, the more arresting—the more successful I think it is. Neutral shades are forgettable. Super-saturated colors excite me because they have the ability to sweep you up and take you away on a journey into another world. I think about the adventure I want to have, and I follow it. There's no reason to be constrained by a limited palette of colors. All the colors are my friends. I don't want any to feel left out! I love mixing and mingling and meandering through a dreamscape of intense shades. In the wrong hands, these colors can crash hard. But with high risk come big rewards—a room so glorious it transports you, or so magical it will make you feel like dancing.

A heightened sensory experience is achieved with a console table that wears a woven skirt. Bright, figural artwork adds just one more layer of quirkiness. It's a humorous painting that jumps off the wall. The secret is to keep going until the fun stops. That's when you know it's time to get off the ride.

TECHNICOLOR DREAM HOUSE

Being bold pays off big in this home, starting with the larger-than-life living room. If the tones are a bit audacious, if the patterns seem a bit reckless, then I have achieved just the right balance. The trick is not to hesitate and not to halt. And never be formulaic. Designing a super-saturated home is similar to conducting an orchestra. You need to hear from every section. One single note — like one single color — lacks range and depth. It doesn't hold your interest. I prefer slight variations that don't quite match. For example, I purposely chose sconce shades that are a different red from the red flowers on the wallpaper behind them. It immediately makes the pairing more riveting. It's like hearing a vibrato in music — a slight variation in pitch that produces a stronger, richer note. The wildly varied colors I mix together add to the depth of the design. When things match too much, the design falls flat. Not matching adds more interest and complexity.

My creative choices in this home are informed by my obsession with the abstract painter Mark Rothko and the strength behind his juxtaposition of large blocks of color. Artists tend to be so much freer with their color combinations than most interior designers. I am happy to embrace their more radical visions in my work.

Luckily, the couple behind this renovation are two of my boldest clients. I knew they would easily follow me into this Technicolor dream. They were eager for me to carry them from reality to fantasy. We started with the walls. The original nineteenth-century boiserie wood paneling in the living room, though glorious, was far too serious. It needed levity and playfulness. We decided to be very

PREVIOUS PAGES: There's a method to my madness. If a home has good bones, strong architectural interest, exquisite moldings, and beautiful proportions, you can pull out all the stops with color. Traditional shapes, the addition of antiques, and inherent classicism give the room balance and make it read chic, not gaudy. But beware—the same colors used somewhere without architectural perfection might look garish. RIGHT: If you're going to go for it, go for it. I can't stand rooms that take one bold moment, such as stunningly blue walls, and then water it down with all-white furniture. Instead, I continue to add the spice: a sofa that looks as though it was inspired by Dorothy's ruby-red slippers. A chair amped up with a Cy Twombly–esque graffiti fabric.

ABOVE: The dining room chairs are intentionally less formal than the mahogany Regency table they surround. They add a whimsical and lighthearted touch to the space. They're hosting their own private little rebellion. I love the way the chairs are so crisp and white against the backdrop of the painterly chinoiserie wallpaper behind them. RIGHT: Through the blue paneled living room, we can see into the dining room, where a beautifully busy pattern is introduced on the walls. The rooms in this apartment are all open to one another. I needed a wallpaper that could hold its own against the uniquely concentrated color in the living room. The pretty flora and fauna of this Schumacher paper provided the perfect respite. With it, I was able to segue from blues to bluish greens, from reds to orangey reds.

"There's no formula for creating a color palette. When it happens, it's just magic."

theatrical and paint the walls a spectacular hue. I imagined something richer, deeper, and even more magical than the actuality of the lake view I saw through their windows. My mind jumped to the sacred Blue City of Jodhpur in India's northwest region of Rajasthan. If a whole city can be swathed in blue, why not just one room?

As I moved through the rest of the apartment, I continued to keep the color volume turned way up. A striking ruby-red sofa here, a lacquered lavender hallway there, orchid-pink drapery in the bedroom, cobalt-blue doors throughout. I'm proud to be known for my passionate mixes of vivid color. I think of it as my superpower. My color choices stir things up and inject energy, joie de vivre, and confidence into every room. There is a limit, of course, but it's important to push yourself. Most people are afraid of going too far, of crossing that line between tasteful and gauche. I will walk right up to that line. I can't tell you where it is, but I know when I get there.

A striking white Fornasetti vase sits atop a table. There's something about having a human face staring back at me. You can sell me anything with a face on it! It always adds life to a room.

The dining room is so large that we were able to create a separate space for a cozy banquette in the same room as the more formal round dining table. The flexibility appeals to me.

LEFT: This hallway is a surprise winner. When I first saw it, it was like a tired old workhorse, dragging you along from the public spaces to the private ones. It was dark, with beige walls and brown stone floors. Honestly, it felt like a punishment just to walk to the bedroom. I had this mad idea to paint the floor with a geometric pattern, but without any obvious repeats. Then we used a pale lavender lacquer on the walls to let light bounce everywhere. ABOVE: As soon as you step off the elevator into this vestibule, you're immediately introduced to a whole new world. You are somewhere *different*. Teeny areas somehow expand in my imagination. I love to be right on the edge of good taste, and small rooms are a great place to push the envelope. I'm drawn to the contrast between the striking blue-lacquered door and the antique late-1700s table mounted to the wall. We used hand-dipped marbleized paper on the walls and ceiling, so the space feels as if it has been gift wrapped.

"Beige is for beginners."

The lady of the house is a fair blonde, and pinks look so pretty on her. I just had to use that color in her bedroom, but we added lots of red for a stronger hit that ties this whole house together. Now the room is more of a nod to Rothko than *Sleeping Beauty*. Each shade of red is slightly different, and none of them match exactly—it's that kind of slightly off-kilter palette that invigorates me. This room gets great light, and we wanted to take advantage of that by using super-saturated, feel-good shades. The shape of the headboard reminds me of a great big kiss. FOLLOWING PAGES: This cozy den covered in Quadrille's Arbre de Matisse wallpaper is the perfect, treehouse-like retreat after a busy day.

Cozy Cocoons

I never walk away from a dark, cramped, overlooked area – a closet, a maid's room, a den, an attic, or a nook. I rush in with everything I've got and turn them into coveted retreats and miniature fantasylands. I've found that tiny, tucked-away areas, if done correctly, can completely envelop you and allow you the luxury of getting lost inside their walls. These forgotten spaces have the potential to become wonderful hideaways and have the ability to wrap you safely inside. Step inside one of these secret refuges and you'll see what I mean. Here, Quadrille's Arbre de Matisse in matching fabric and wallpaper invites you to hide out from the rest of the world in your own private enchanted forest.

LEFT: When you have an ugly-duckling space, the name of the game is distraction. The busy matching prints recede into one another. The unexpected use of brown takes the retreat a step farther away from the brighter, bolder hues seen everywhere else in the apartment. ABOVE LEFT: A mom's hideout is plush with silky carpeting and indulgent with a cozy mohair sectional. Here, there are no noisy children, no messes— just space to breathe. ABOVE RIGHT: What better place for a mounted sailfish than in this TV den? The blue-on-blue Pierre Frey tree of life pattern creates the perfect backdrop.

SERIOUSLY SEDUCTIVE

A secret garden waits for you inside this incredible apartment. My whole design concept started in the living room, with an enchanting, hand-painted Japanese mountain-scape wallpaper covered in a riot of cherry blossoms. The paper had been on my mind forever. I was obsessed with it, but it needed just the right space to work well. Finally, I was able to use it when we designed this spectacular home. One look, and you are left wondering: "Do I stay here in the real world or slip into the dream?" The answer is easy.

This apartment is one of my all-time-favorite projects, in part because I was able to work with a very unusual palette of super-saturated greens. My design relies on shades that are a little off. Every color I used here is powerful: jades, teals, aquas, cinnamons, citrons, and ochers. I want people to be enchanted at every turn. The connected colors carry you through the apartment, but they don't repeat. The range of hues is what makes them thrilling.

Odd color combos are energizing. I have an emotional reaction to each new mash-up of fabrics, patterns, and colors that I put together. When the right mix reveals itself, it smacks me upside the head. The end result is an apartment that is sultry, luxurious, and strong. All the elements of the design are incredibly seductive. Fluted columns, tufted tassels, mohair throws, and velvet pillows make the "more is more" case. The textures in the apartment range from beautiful terrazzo inlaid floors to leather doors to cinnamon-spice damask walls.

This palette can't help but conjure up thoughts of the French designer Madeleine Castaing. She was definitely top of mind when wielding teal and aqua shades with such bravado. We painted all the doors a dark teal as a form of punctuation as you move from room to room. Every change keeps things a little off balance. This bold apartment doesn't shy away from attention.

LEFT: The foyer is an ode to Madeleine Castaing. The patterns look like they were pulled from the 1940s, almost to a T. Because the hallway receives little natural light, we had to be inventive. We designed a giant custom-made mirror and placed it on a wall opposite the opening to the den, which overlooks the lake. It helps to reflect light into an otherwise dark entry. For added shine, the original polished terrazzo tile has brass inlays. The entry was large enough to house an alluring 1940s vintage dining table, perfect for overflow at large dinner parties. A pendant of amethyst glass amid the teals is one of those pairings that confirms there is such a thing as love at first sight.
ABOVE: The striped wallpaper is capped by floral paper on the ceiling. Top-to-bottom perfection.

PREVIOUS PAGES: The living room is lively and loose, with all the right ingredients for a good time. An ocher mohair sofa and curved bentwood chairs create a chic grouping in front of the fireplace, while the diagonally striped velvet sofa and games table move guests in a decidedly more festive direction. I had never done two separate and novel sofas back-to-back, and I am so happy with the result. Good design springs from experimentation. It's more about what moves you than what you can explain rationally. ABOVE: An oversize circular hammered-brass sconce appears like the sun rising over the mountains. RIGHT: A row of rotary dimmer light switches is practically a work of art. FAR RIGHT: A ladies writing desk is one thing, but when it's covered in jade-dyed goatskin—it's no one's lady.